You, Me, & Our
Once Upon A Times

WestBow Press books may be ordered through booksellers or by contacting:

WestBow Press
A Division of Thomas Nelson & Zondervan
1663 Liberty Drive
Bloomington, IN 47403
www.westbowpress.com
1 (866) 928-1240

Because of the dynamic nature of the Internet, any web addresses or links contained in this book may have changed since publication and may no longer be valid. The views expressed in this work are solely those of the author and do not necessarily reflect the views of the publisher, and the publisher hereby disclaims any responsibility for them.

Any people depicted in stock imagery provided by Thinkstock are models, and such images are being used for illustrative purposes only.
Certain stock imagery © Thinkstock.

Interior Graphics: Miriam Jeannette Douglas

Scripture quotations taken from the Holy Bible, New Living Translation, Copyright © 1996, 2004. Used by permission of Tyndale House Publishers, Inc., Wheaton, Illinois 60189. All rights reserved.

This book is a work of non-fiction. Unless otherwise noted, the author and the publisher make no explicit guarantees as to the accuracy of the information contained in this book and in some cases, names of people and places have been altered to protect their privacy.

ISBN: 978-1-5127-4674-7 (sc)
ISBN: 978-1-5127-4899-4 (hc)
ISBN: 978-1-5127-4675-4 (e)

Library of Congress Control Number: 2016911017

Print Information Available on Last Page

WestBow Press rev. date: 11/14/2016

WESTBOW
P R E S S*
A DIVISION OF THOMAS NELSON
& ZONDERVAN

You, Me, & Our Once Upon A Times

written by

Michelle Branza

illustrated by
Miriam Douglas

About the Author

Michelle Aranza is a momma of 5 strong boys and one beautiful daughter. She clearly models how a godly woman graciously speaks truth, walks in courage, and wholeheartedly loves those entrusted to her leadership.

Michelle is the founder of Arise Women's Conference and the Project Hope Foundation. In addition to all these things, she and her husband, Jacob, bring oversight to a family of flourishing churches.

"You have not chosen one another, but I have chosen you for one another."
— C.S. Lewis, The Four Loves

ever has there ever been a child
so loved, so adored, so cherished!

Never before in ALL of history and as far as I can
see, when I look really hard, for
really long ... I see none.

It all began a long time ago in a place quite near
when all of heaven stopped and took note of YOU !

The you that was
and the you that was yet to be
... the ALL of you!

It's as though I heard the angels say, "WOW!"

Psalm 91:11

There are 8 billion people in the whole world but only 1 of them is YOU...

and this is where "OUR" Once Upon a Times began!

You see, to you, you're just YOU.
But to them & to anyone with eyes you are

brighter than the brightest star...
braver than the bravest lion...
and sweeter than a cherry pie.

Because you truly are a One of a Kind,
kinda Wonder!

Simply Breathtaking!

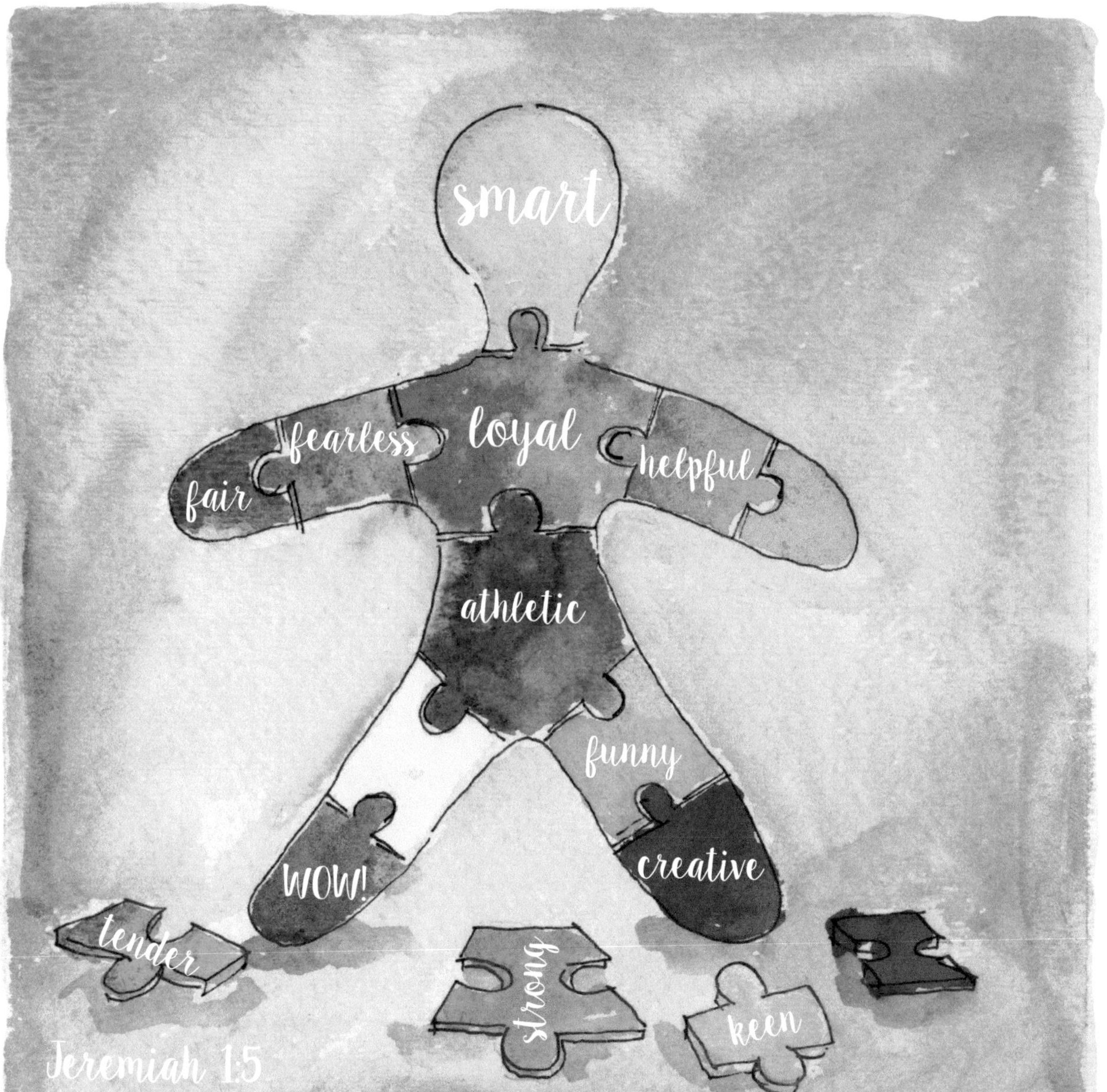
smart
fearless
loyal
fair
helpful
athletic
funny
WOW!
creative
tender
strong
keen
Jeremiah 1:5

I knew you were something special the moment I first saw your beautiful face!

When our eyes met for the very first time the course of my life was changed forever and just so YOU know-

I've never looked back!

Isaiah 6:3

Everything about you became monumental!

Your first coo, first smile, first steps-
all of your firsts were like the firsts of my whole
world because...

...there's only ONE you!

Everything we've shared and everything we will
share are all "OUR" Once Upon a Times.

I wish I could see the invisible string that ties us together. I find it curious and wonder how it works that when you smile, I'm happy and when you hurt, I actually feel your pain...

...How can this be?

I'm thinking that OUR Once Upon A Times must have begun before we ever met...

... Amazing!

Hmmm, I wonder how it is that my heart was one size for all my life, until I met YOU, that is!

Then it began growing and, yes, I did feel it grow and grow and grow because of you, and with you -

My heart is BIGGER!

Thank you, thank you, thank you for all the Once Upon A Times we've shared and those we've yet to share!

A. 2006

H. 1999

W. 1995

J. 1991

C. 1986

J. 1983

1 Corinthians 13:13

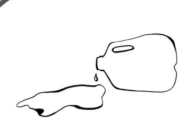

Some days have been the BEST and some have felt

just awful

Some have been as though they were sent from heaven,
and some have made our hearts ache!

However, they are, at the end of the day...
...ALL OURS!

Altogether, they're "OUR" storybook
moments and that's what makes them best of
ALL.

He is the Author of THIS story,
and the best is yet to come!

Promises For Your Heart

You are delighted in.

Isaiah 49:16 NLT
"I have written your name on the palms of my hands. Always in my mind is a picture of you."

You are protected.

Psalm 91:11 NLT
"For he will order his angels to protect you wherever you go."

You are a masterpiece.

Ephesians 2:10 NLT
"For we are God's masterpiece. He has created us anew in Christ Jesus, so we can do the good things he planned for us long ago."

You have a unique purpose.

Jeremiah 29:11 NLT
"For I know the plans I have for you," says the Lord. "They are plans for good and not for disaster, to give you a future and a hope."

God fills your heart with love.

Romans 5:5 NLT
"And this hope will not lead to disappointment. For we know how dearly God loves us, because he has given us the Holy Spirit to fill our hearts with his love."

God is the Author of YOUR story.

Psalm 139:16 NLT
"You saw me before I was born. Every day of my life was recorded in your book. Every moment was laid out before a single day had passed."

My precious children,

I wrote this book for you - unaware how quickly the days would pass.

Our Once Upon A Times have been numbered, and I'm forever grateful that mine are filled with you. ♡

our Story continues...

Printed in the United States
By Bookmasters